Common Core Lessons & Activities:
Political Parties and Elections

By Carole Marsh
Published by Gallopade International, Inc.

Printed in the U.S.A. (Peachtree City, Georgia)

TABLE OF CONTENTS

G: Includes Graphic Organizer
GO: Graphic Organizer is also available 8½" x 11" online download at www.gallopade.com/client/go
(numbers above correspond to the graphic organizer numbers online)

READING INFORMATIONAL TEXT

Purpose of Political Parties

Read the text and answer the questions.

Political parties are made up of groups of people who share similar beliefs and opinions. People support a political party that has the same values and ideas as they do. Large political parties may have many millions of members.

The main purpose of political parties is to win elections, to be in charge of the government, and to influence government policies.

The two major political parties in the United States are the Democratic Party and the Republican Party. Other parties exist, but they do not have as much influence as the two major parties. Having more than one party ensures that different ideas get heard.

Political parties clearly establish their views on specific issues. Members of political parties work to get people from their party elected to public office. Information from the media, Internet, speeches, rallies, advertising, email, posters, and even yard signs all help political parties get their message to the voters and support their candidate. Once candidates from a political party are elected, the party hopes that laws will be passed that support the party's positions on issues.

1. A. Use a dictionary to define policies as it is used in the text.
   B. What is a "government policy"?
2. A. Use a dictionary to define influence as it is used in the text.
   B. Who or what do political parties want to influence?
3. Summarize the main idea of the text.
4. How do people choose a political party to support? Cite evidence from the text to support your answer.
5. Why do political parties want to get people from their party elected to public office?
6. Use online resources to research someone who has recently been elected to public office. Find out what political party they belong to and how their stand on the issues matched their party's beliefs.

READING INFORMATIONAL TEXT

The Democratic Party

Read the text and answer the questions.

The Democratic Party is the oldest political party that still exists today. Andrew Jackson was the first U.S. president from the Democratic Party. The donkey is the unofficial symbol of the Democratic Party. It was first used to describe President Jackson as not very smart. However, he used it to represent the hard work and strong will of his political party.

The Democratic Party has changed in many ways since it was founded. In the 1800s, Democrats supported slavery and states' rights. During the Civil War, the Democratic Party disagreed over many issues and split into Northern Democrats and Southern Democrats. This split helped Republican candidate Abraham Lincoln to win the presidency.

After the Civil War, the Democratic Party began to change their position on many issues. Democrats today are often known as "liberals" or "progressives." Democratic Party members are typically open to change and not bound by traditional values. Democrats believe the government has a big role in taking care of the people. They support government programs to help people solve their problems.

Some of the best-known Democratic U.S. presidents include Franklin D. Roosevelt, John F. Kennedy, and Barack Obama. Franklin D. Roosevelt introduced the New Deal to help Americans recover from the Great Depression. John F. Kennedy supported the black civil rights movement. In 2008, Barack Obama was elected the first black President of the United States.

1. Define liberals and progressives as they are used in the text.
2. Explain how a divided Democrat Party helped Abraham Lincoln win the presidency. Use logical reasoning to support your answer.
3. Use online and classroom resources to research the New Deal. What can you infer about why the New Deal encouraged big government?
4. Use online sources to research the Democratic Party today. Describe the party's stand on today's issues. Proofread and edit your work.

The Republican Party

Read the text and answer the questions.

The Republican Party was founded in 1854. Republicans opposed slavery and supported a united country unity over individual states' rights. Most Republican support was in the northern United States.

After the Civil War, Republicans dominated the White House for more than 50 years. Only a few Democratic presidents were elected during that time.

The Republican Party is nicknamed the "GOP." That stands for the "Grand Old Party" or "Gallant Old Party." The symbol of the party is the elephant. It came from an 1874 political cartoon making fun of political parties. To many Republicans, it symbolizes strength and intelligence.

Republicans today are often known as "conservatives." They believe in upholding traditional values. Republicans believe in smaller government and lower taxes. They believe people do better when they solve their own problems rather than rely on government programs.

Some of the best-known Republican presidents include Abraham Lincoln, Theodore Roosevelt, and Ronald Reagan. President Lincoln guided the U.S. through the Civil War. Theodore Roosevelt watched over the building of the Panama Canal. Ronald Reagan led America into a time of great economic prosperity.

1. A. Use a dictionary to define conservatives as it is used in the text.
   B. Use a dictionary to define economic prosperity.
2. A. Infer why most Republican support was in the northern U.S. during the 1850s.
   B. From what you know about the Civil War, infer why Republicans dominated the U.S. presidency after the Civil War.
3. Do you think people might do better solving their own problems rather than relying on government programs? Discuss in class.
4. Use online sources to research the Republican Party today. Describe the party's stand on today's issues. Proofread and edit your work.

COMPARE AND CONTRAST

Republicans and Democrats

Complete the graphic organizer by comparing and contrasting the Republican and Democratic Party platforms.

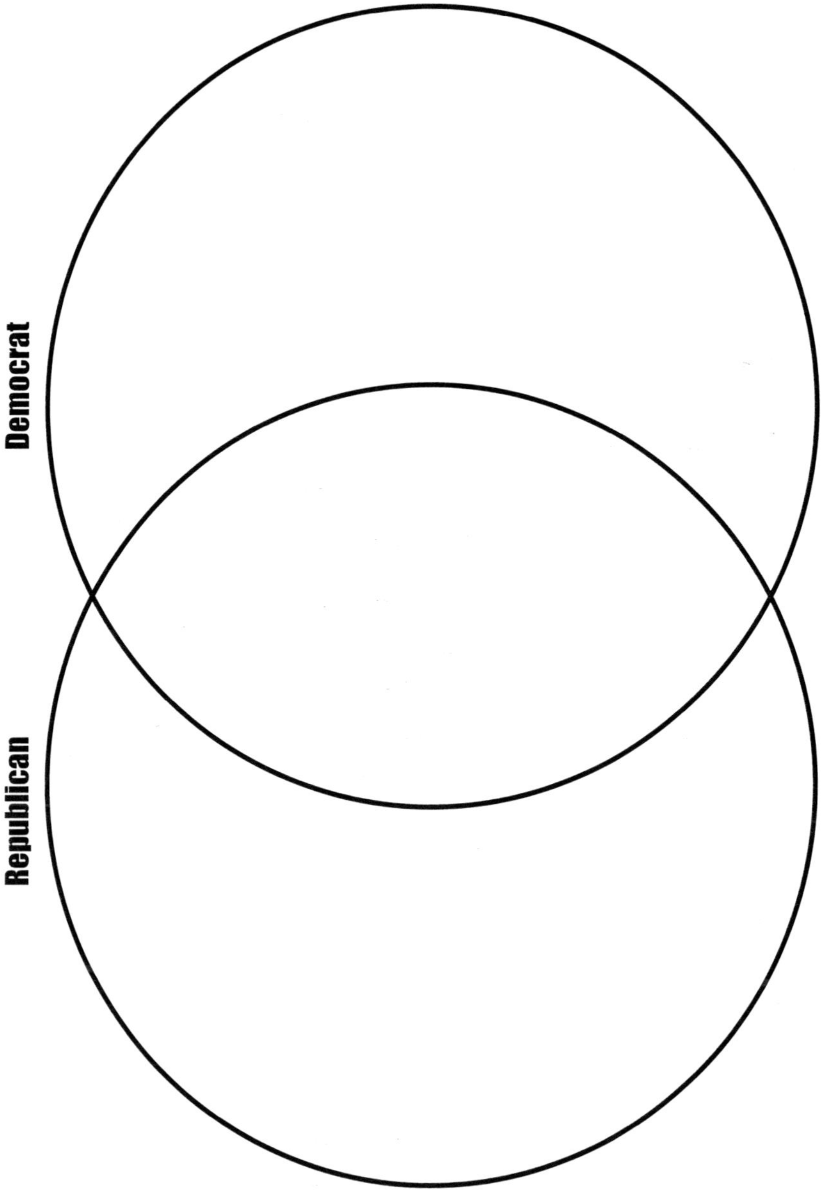

The Role of Third Parties

Read the text and answer the questions.

The United States operates on a two-party system made up of the Republican and Democratic parties. However, other political parties can present candidates for government offices. These political parties are called "third parties."

Third parties usually develop when groups of people have specific issues they care about and want to fight for. For example, the Jobless Party formed in 1932. Its goal was to bring attention to the many people without jobs during the Great Depression. In 1970, people who wanted increased individual rights formed the Libertarian Party. The Libertarian Party still exists today.

While third parties have not succeeded in getting a presidential candidate elected, they can have a powerful influence on politics. They bring attention to specific issues that might otherwise be overlooked. Third parties can also have a major effect on a presidential election by taking support from Republican or Democratic candidates. They can also boost another party's candidates by endorsing them and their policies.

1. A. Define endorsing as it is used in the text. Find a synonym.
   B. Infer how a third party could help another party's candidate by endorsing him or her.
2. Describe several ways that third parties can influence government. Cite evidence from the text to support your answer.
3. Divide into groups. Use classroom and online resources to research other third parties in United States history. Find out how these parties changed government policies, brought awareness to specific issues, or influenced political elections. Create a computer presentation with graphics to present to the class. Discuss your findings.
4. Have you heard of the "Tea Party"? The Tea Party is a political movement, not an official political party. Use online resources to research the Tea Party. Write a blog about their role in politics today.
5. Create an imaginary third party around a cause that's important to you. Create a poster advertising it, and write a narrative to describe it..

Political Parties and Elections Vocabulary

Use a dictionary and other resources to complete the graphic organizer for each vocabulary word.

absentee ballot	convention	liberal
ballot	delegate	nominee
bipartisan	electorate	platform
campaign	GOP	poll
conservative	incumbent	primary

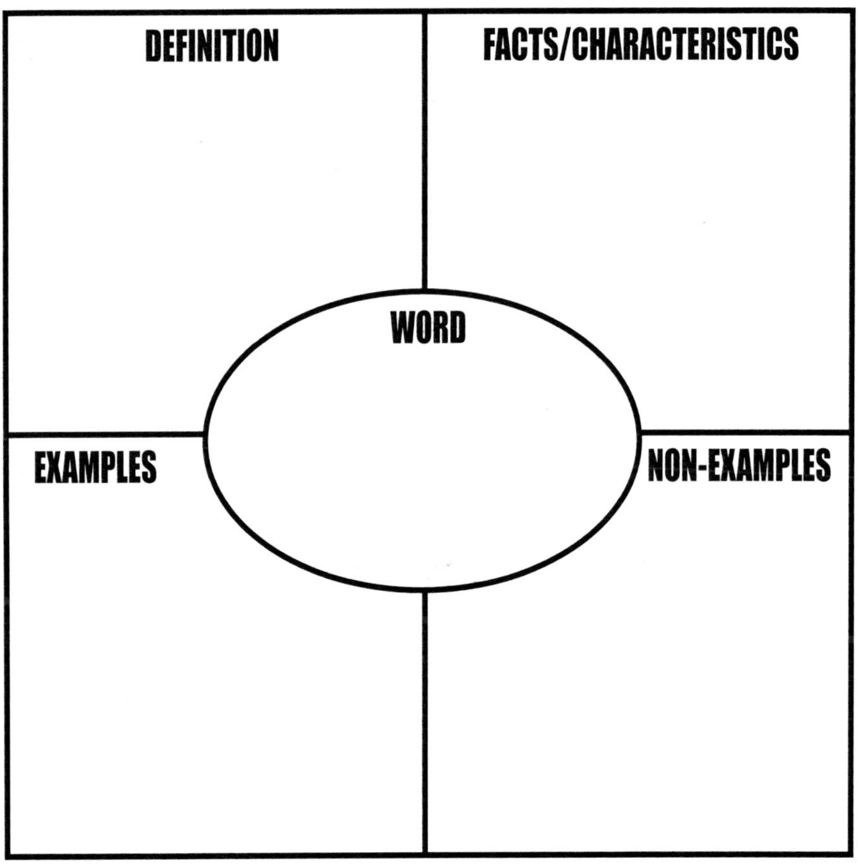

MAP ACTIVITY

Electoral College

Look at the Electoral College map. Use a map of the U.S. to label the states that are not labeled. Then, answer the questions.

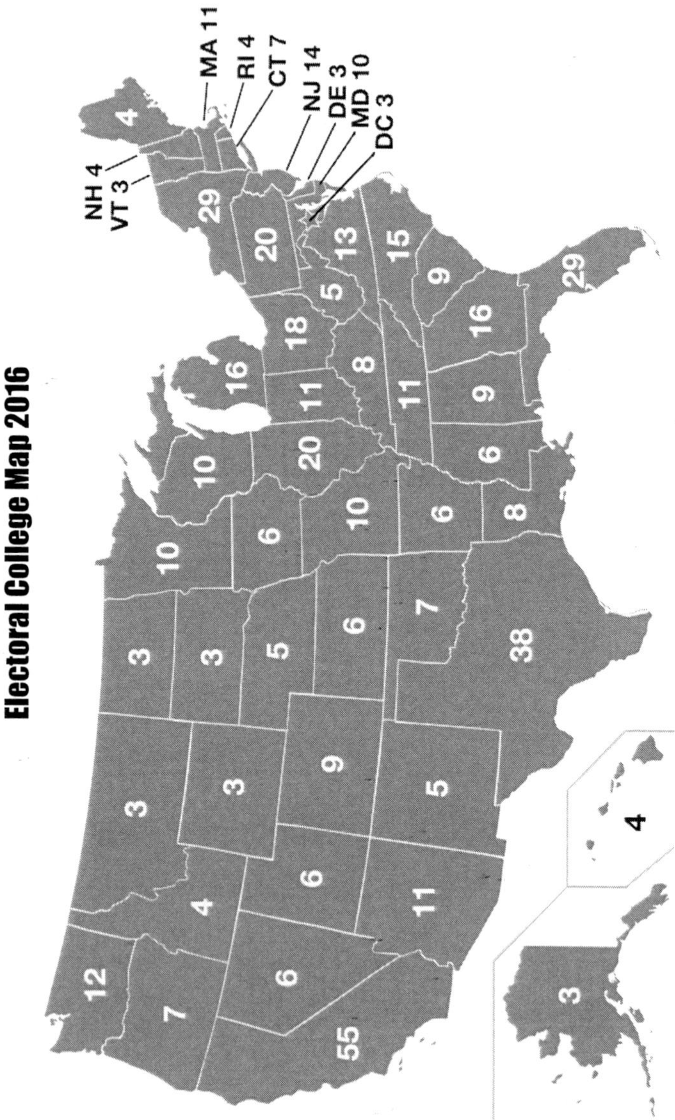

PART A: Use the map to determine whether each statement is true or false.

1. _____ Texas has the most Electoral College votes.
2. _____ The number of Electoral College votes depends on the physical size of the state.
3. _____ Each state has at least two Electoral College votes.
4. _____ Residents of Washington, D.C., are not represented in the Electoral College.

PART B: Use the map and your research of the Electoral College to identify which state is being described.

5. This state has 13 Representatives and 2 Senators in the U.S. Congress.
6. This state has the most Electoral College votes.
7. This small East Coast state has a large population. It has 12 Representatives and 2 Senators in the U.S. Congress.

PART C: Make inferences from the map and your research of the Electoral College to answer the questions.

8. Name the six states that have the most electoral votes.
9. Explain why a U.S. presidential candidate wins the election if he or she gains at least 270 Electoral College votes.
10. Swing states are states that do not traditionally vote for a certain political party. Common swing states include Ohio and Florida. Explain why presidential candidates might spend more time campaigning in swing states.
11. Knowing that the amount of Electoral College votes are based on each state's population, what can you infer about how a census could affect a presidential election?
12. In your opinion, is it a good policy to base the number of Electoral College votes on the population of a state? Why or why not? Support your answer with logical reasoning.

PRIMARY SOURCE ANALYSIS

Summer Schedule

This political cartoon was published in 1947. It shows Senator Robert A. Taft looking at the electoral map to plan his "summer schedule" of campaigning. He was hoping to win the Republican nomination for U.S. President for the 1948 election.

Analyze the political cartoon and answer the questions.

Courtesy of the National Archives

1. Predict which states Senator Taft will be sure to visit. Why?
2. Why is visiting a state in person an effective way for a candidate to win votes?
3. Senator Taft would not compete in the primaries until the following spring. Why do you think he wanted to campaign during the summer?
4. Compare the map in the cartoon to the electoral vote map on page 8. Compare the states where you can read the numbers. Make a chart comparing the electoral vote numbers of 1948 to those of 2016. Discuss your results in class. Which states gained electoral votes? Why? Did any states lose electoral votes? If so, why?

Electoral College

Use online and classroom resources to complete the graphic organizer. Describe the problem solved by the Electoral College.

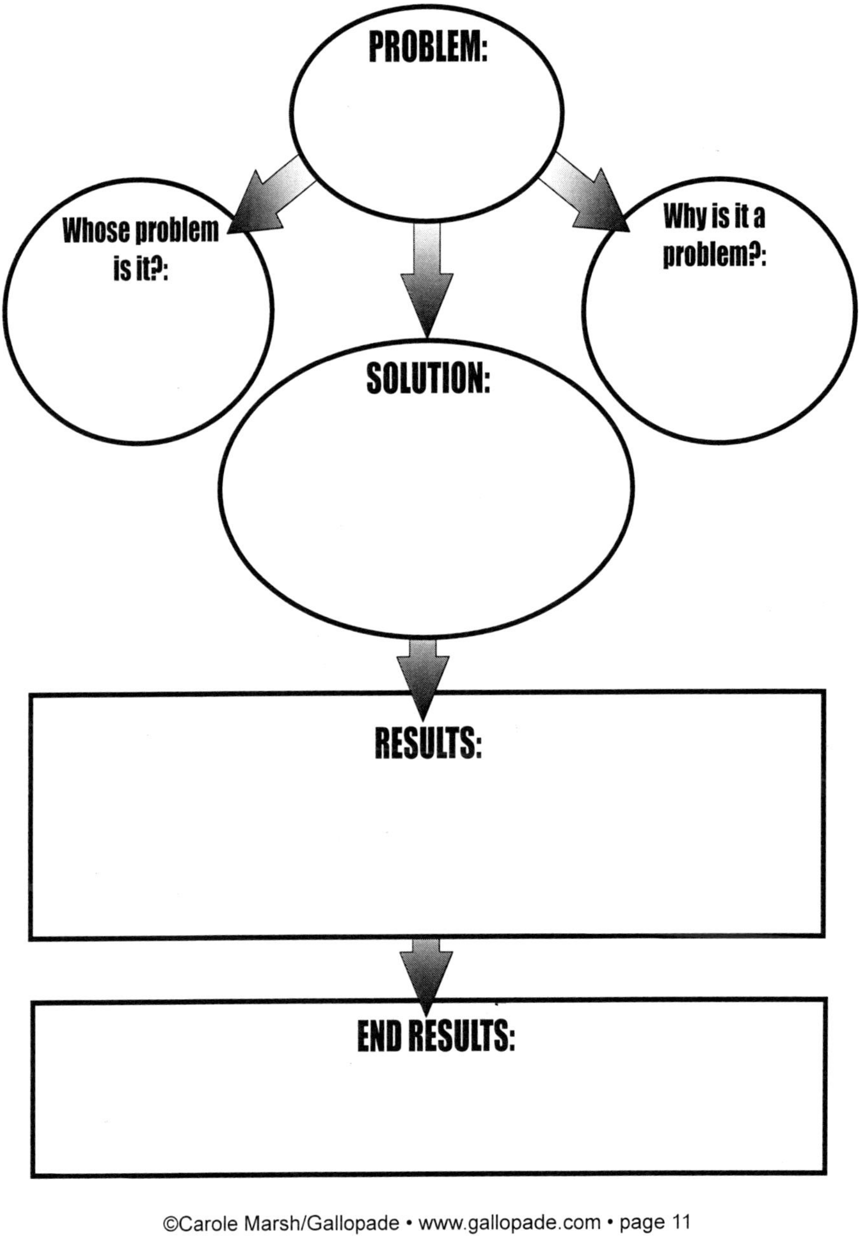

Steps to Elect the President

Complete the graphic organizer by putting the following events in chronological order. Label what time of year each event takes place. Use specific dates when possible.

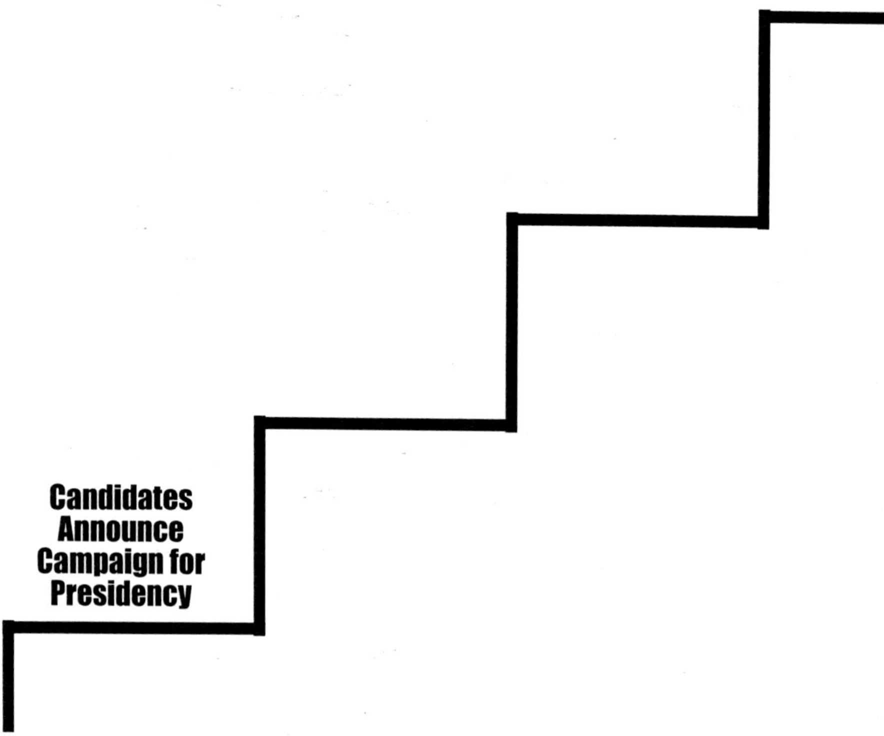

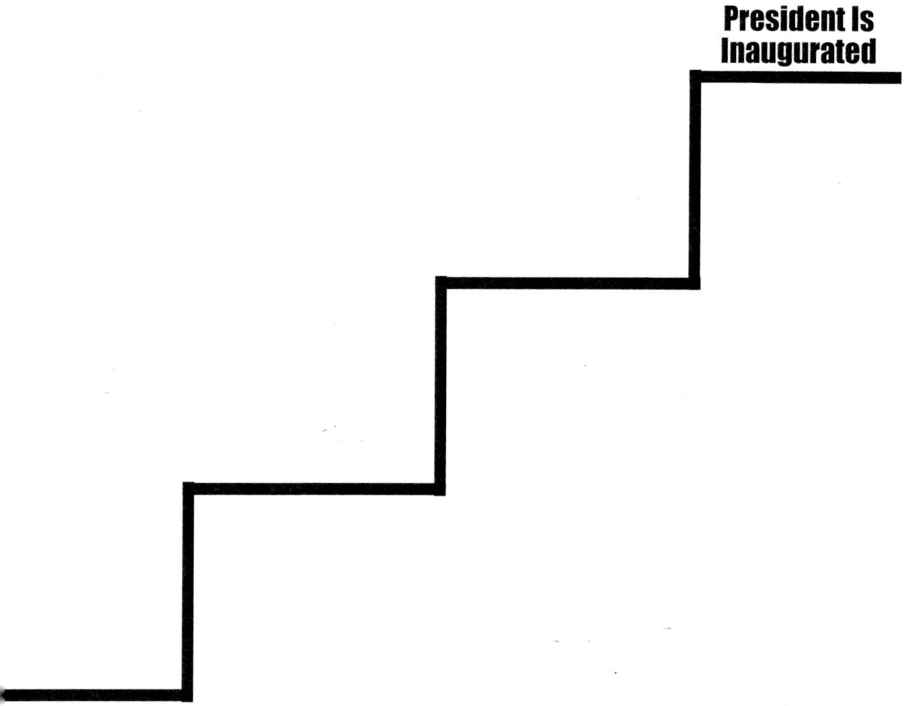

Word Bank

Citizens Vote

Candidates Campaign for Their Party's Nomination

Nominee Announced at Party Conventions

Electoral College Votes

Primary Elections

Campaign Poster

Look at the campaign poster and answer the questions.

1. Who is the intended audience of this poster?
2. The poster compares the state of the country at the end of President Hoover's administration to what President Roosevelt accomplished after he was elected. Describe the differences in the following:
   A. Bread lines vs. higher wages
   B. Homeless vs. low rent homes
   C. Banks closed vs. Social Security (define Social Security in your answer)
3. What can you infer from the poster about how Americans felt in 1932 vs. 1940? Cite evidence from the poster.
4. Do you think this poster succeeds at convincing voters to reelect Roosevelt? Why or why not?

The Role of Media in Elections

Read the text and answer the questions.

The media is essential to a democratic election. Citizens who have the right to vote need to have information about candidates and issues. In order to make informed decisions, voters can learn from many types of media including newspapers, television, radio, magazines, and the Internet.

The media gives voters information about people running for office and where they stand on specific issues. It reports on party conventions, debates between candidates, local campaigns across the country, and other events.

The media presents information in several ways. Sometimes the media is objective, offering factual news reports. Other times, the media is subjective, offering opinions through political cartoons and editorials. Because of that, voters need to read, listen to, and/or watch many different media sources. Voters can analyze the information they learn from all media sources to create their own opinions about candidates and issues.

A fair and balanced media is essential in any nation. The media has a very important responsibility to be unbiased and fair. That responsibility is particularly important in a democratic country where the people hold the power by voting, and get their information from the media.

1. A. Use a dictionary to define objective as used in the text. Find several synonyms.
   B. Use a print media source to identify an objective article. Present the article to the class and discuss why it is objective.
2. A. Use a dictionary to define subjective as it is used in the text.
   B. Use the Internet to identify a subjective article. Present the article to the class and discuss why it is subjective.
3. In your own words, explain why media is essential for democratic elections. Predict what can happen when the media is biased. Discuss as a class.

GRAPHIC ANALYSIS

Requirements to Become a U.S. Politician

Complete the graphic organizer by filling in the requirements needed for election to each office in the U.S. government.

U.S. President	U.S. Senator	U.S. Representative
1.	1.	1.
2.	2.	2.
3.	3.	3.

DATA ANALYSIS

Voter Turnout

Study the chart and answer the questions.

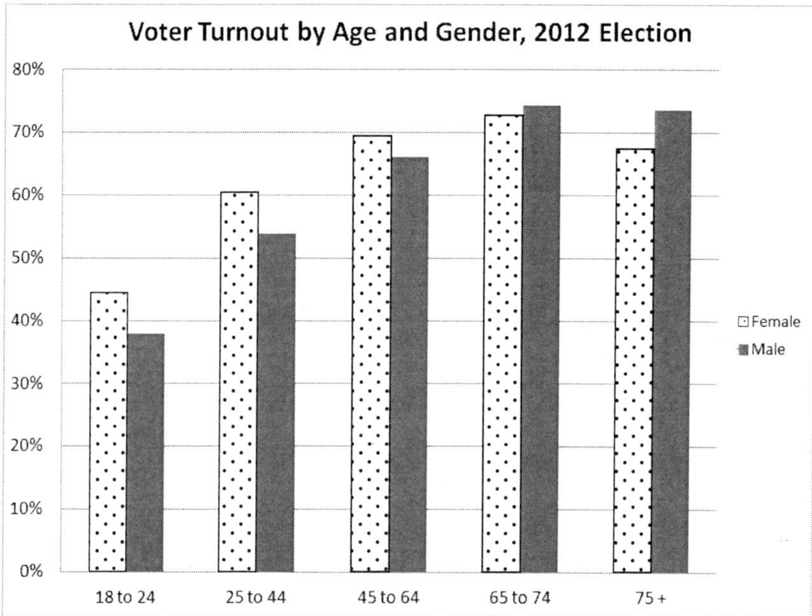

Courtesy of the Hartford Courant

1. What is the purpose of this chart?
2. Which gender age 25-44 voted more in the 2012 election?
3. What percentage of male voters age 45-64 voted in the 2012 election?
4. Which age and gender voted the least in the 2012 election?
5. Which age group had the most similar percentage of male and female voters?
6. In your opinion, did age or gender most affect voter turnout? Cite evidence from the chart to support your answer.
7. Why do you think voters age 65 and above have the highest turnout? Why do younger voters have the lowest turnout? Discuss as a class.

Campaign Slogans

Use online resources to complete the table. Identify which presidential candidate used each slogan and explain how the slogan described their campaign.

Slogan	President	Explanation
"Don't Swap Horses in the Middle of the Stream"	1864	
"Happy Days Are Here Again"	1932	
"The Stakes Are Too High for You to Stay Home"	1964	
"Are You Better Off than You Were Four Years Ago?"	1980	

2000 Presidental Election

Read the text and answer the questions.

The 2000 Presidential election was one of the closest races in history. Republican Governor George W. Bush ran against Democratic Vice President Al Gore.

The election all came down to Florida. Votes were so close that Florida law called for a recount. Machines electronically recounted the ballots and gave Bush a lead of only 327 votes out of the almost 6 million votes cast in Florida.

The Florida Supreme Court ordered that votes from certain counties be counted by hand. The reason was that many of the Florida ballots were unclear because voters had to manually punch out a small circle of paper next to their candidate choice. Some of the punch marks did not work properly.

As the counties submitted their hand recount results, Bush's lead decreased to only 200 votes. The recounts by hand took a very long time. The U.S. Supreme Court became involved. They ruled that the recounts had to stop. Their decision meant that George Bush won the election by a narrow margin of votes.

In the end, Bush won 271 Electoral College votes, just one more than he needed to win. Al Gore received more popular votes than Bush but only 266 Electoral College votes. The 2000 election was the first time since 1888 that a president lost the popular vote but won the Electoral College vote.

1. What can you infer from the text about why Florida state law would require a machine recount in this election?
2. What are potential dangers of hand counting votes? Do you agree with the U.S. Supreme Court's decision to throw out the recounts?
3. Explain how a national election can be affected so much by one state. Use your knowledge of the Electoral College to support your answer.
4. Explain how a candidate can lose the popular vote but win the Electoral College vote. According to this information, do you think Bush should have won the election? Why or why not?

PRIMARY SOURCE ANALYSIS

Importance of Voting

Read the quotes and answer the questions.

"Every election is determined by the people who show up."

– Larry Sabato

"The only way to change is to vote. People are responsible."

– Paul Wellstone

"Nobody will ever <u>deprive</u> the American people of the right to vote except the American people themselves and the only way they could do this is by not voting."

– Franklin D. Roosevelt

1. A. Summarize the main idea of each quote.
   B. Summarize the main idea of all three quotes.
2. A. Use a dictionary to define <u>deprive</u>. List 2-3 synonyms.
3. Use online resources to research 3-5 reasons why citizens might not vote. State your opinion about each reason you list. Is it a valid reason not to vote?
4. A. Divide into groups. Each group will choose a state (one group must choose your state). Use online resources to research the requirements to vote in that state. Create a poster to list the requirements.
   B. Compare the state requirements. Why do you think these requirements are in place? Discuss in class.

Campaign Costs

Political campaigns are very expensive. This chart compares the campaign costs of candidates running for Congress to the campaign costs of presidential candidates. Candidates spend money on media, travel, campaign events, and other items. Campaign costs have increased greatly in the last few decades.

Analyze the chart and answer the questions.

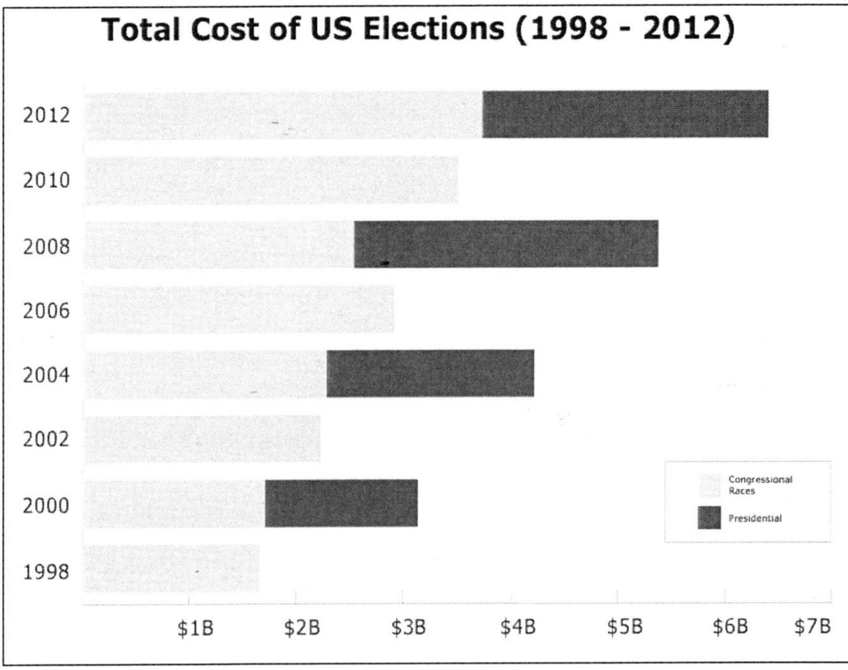

1. What year had the lowest presidential campaign costs?
2. What year had the overall highest campaign costs?
3. Why are Congressional campaign costs more expensive than presidential campaign costs? Is there one year where that was not the case?
4. A. Use online resources to determine why campaign costs are increasing. Create a computer presentation of your findings.
   B. Make predictions about campaign costs in the next presidential race. Can you think of any solutions to the problem? Discuss in class.

Why Elections Matter

Read the fictional narrative and answer the questions.

Dear Local Representative,

I was upset to hear that our local schools have cut the number of art and music classes offered. My children have always loved band and chorus. In fact, both of them sang in this year's school choral concert. They also loved the painting class. My son is a talented artist. His ability has improved greatly since he took that class at school.

It does not seem fair to take these options from my children's education. Unfortunately, I did not have time to vote on the issue in the last election. What can you do to change this policy?

Sincerely,

A Concerned Parent

Dear Concerned Parent,

I am also very disappointed that music and art classes are being cut in our local schools. The election held last month gave each citizen the opportunity to vote against this decision. Unfortunately, voter turnout was low, and the extra funding bill for schools did not pass. I would encourage you to vote whenever you can in local and national elections to make sure your voice is heard.

Thank you for contacting me. As your representative, I will always do my best to fight for your goals and concerns.

Sincerely,

Your Local Representative

1. Summarize the situation described in the narrative above.
2. A. What was the effect of the Concerned Parent not voting in the recent local election?
   B. Predict what could have happened if many more concerned parents had voted in the local election.
3. Complete the graphic organizer to show why every vote counts.

Cause	→	Effect	→	Effect	→	Fewer art/music classes

PRIMARY SOURCE ANALYSIS

Right to Vote for Women

For many years, it was illegal for American women to vote in any election. Women had to fight for the right to vote. On August 18, 1920, the 19th Amendment to the U.S. Constitution granted women the right to vote.

Study the poster and answer the questions.

Courtesy of Library of Congress

1. What is the purpose of this poster?
2. Who is the intended audience for this poster?
3. Rewrite the text of the poster in your own words. Write your text in the same way: four separate lines.
4. Describe how the illustration supports the message of the poster.

Correlations to Common Core State Standards

For your convenience, correlations are listed page-by-page and for the entire book!

This book is correlated to the Common Core State Standards for English Language Arts grades 3-8, and to Common Core State Standards for Literacy in History, Science, & Technological Subjects grades 6-8.

Correlations are highlighted in gray.

(Highlighted correlations are shown in bold below.)

PAGE #	READING *Includes:* RI: Reading Informational Text RH: Reading History	WRITING *Includes:* W: Writing WHST: Writing History, Science, & Technology	LANGUAGE *Includes:* L: Language LF: Language Foundational Skills	SPEAKING & LISTENING *Includes:* SL: Speaking & Listening
2	RI RH . **1** **2** 3 **4** 5 6 7 **8** 9 **10**	W WHST . 1 **2** 3 **4** 5 6 **7** **8** 9 **10**	L LF . 1 2 3 **4** 5 **6**	SL . 1 2 3 4 5 6
3	RI RH . **1** 2 **3** **4** 5 **6** 7 8 9 **10**	W WHST . 1 **2** 3 **4** **5** **6** **7** **8** **9** **10**	L LF . 1 2 3 **4** 5 **6**	SL . 1 2 3 4 5 6
4	RI RH . **1** 2 **3** **4** 5 **6** 7 8 **9** **10**	W WHST . 1 **2** 3 **4** **5** 6 **7** **8** **9** **10**	L LF . 1 2 3 4 5 6	SL . **1** 2 3 **4** 5 **6**
5	RI RH . 1 2 3 4 5 6 **7** 8 **9** 10	W WHST . 1 2 3 **4** 5 6 7 8 9 **10**	L LF . 1 2 3 4 5 **6**	SL . 1 2 3 4 5 6
6	RI RH . **1** 2 **3** **4** **5** 6 **7** 8 **9** **10**	W WHST . 1 **2** **3** **4** 5 **6** **7** **8** 9 **10**	L LF . 1 2 3 **4** **5** **6**	SL . **1** 2 3 **4** **5** 6
7	RI RH . 1 2 3 **4** 5 6 7 8 9 **10**	W WHST . 1 2 3 4 5 6 7 8 9 10	L LF . 1 2 3 **4** 5 **6**	SL . 1 2 3 4 5 6
8-9	RI RH . **1** 2 3 4 5 6 **7** 8 9 10	W WHST . **1** 2 3 **4** 5 6 7 8 **9** **10**	L LF . 1 2 3 4 5 **6**	SL . 1 2 3 4 5 6
10	RI RH . **1** 2 **3** 4 5 6 **7** 8 9 **10**	W WHST . 1 **2** 3 **4** 5 6 **7** 8 9 **10**	L LF . 1 2 3 4 5 6	SL . **1** **2** 3 **4** **5** 6
11	RI RH . 1 2 3 4 **5** 6 **7** 8 9 10	W WHST . 1 **2** 3 **4** 5 6 **7** 8 9 10	L LF . 1 2 3 4 5 6	SL . 1 2 3 4 5 6
12-13	RI RH . 1 2 3 4 **5** 6 **7** 8 9 10	W WHST . 1 2 3 4 5 6 **7** 8 9 10	L LF . 1 2 3 4 5 6	SL . 1 2 3 4 5 6
14	RI RH . **1** 2 **3** **4** **5** 6 **7** **8** 9 10	W WHST . **1** **2** 3 **4** 5 6 7 8 9 **10**	L LF . 1 2 3 **4** **5** **6**	SL . 1 2 3 4 5 6
15	RI RH . **1** 2 3 **4** 5 **6** 7 8 **9** **10**	W WHST . 1 **2** 3 **4** 5 6 **7** **8** **9** **10**	L LF . 1 2 3 **4** 5 **6**	SL . **1** **2** 3 **4** 5 6
16	RI RH . 1 2 3 4 5 6 **7** 8 9 10	W WHST . 1 **2** 3 **4** 5 6 **7** 8 9 10	L LF . 1 2 3 4 5 6	SL . 1 2 3 4 5 6
17	RI RH . **1** 2 3 4 5 6 **7** 8 9 10	W WHST . **1** 2 3 **4** 5 6 **7** 8 9 10	L LF . 1 2 3 4 5 6	SL . **1** 2 3 **4** 5 6
18	RI RH . 1 2 3 4 5 6 **7** 8 9 10	W WHST . 1 **2** 3 **4** 5 6 **7** 8 9 10	L LF . 1 2 3 **4** **5** 6	SL . 1 2 3 4 5 6
19	RI RH . **1** 2 **3** 4 5 6 7 8 9 **10**	W WHST . **1** **2** 3 **4** 5 6 7 8 9 **10**	L LF . 1 2 3 4 **5** **6**	SL . 1 2 3 4 5 6
20	RI RH . 1 **2** 3 **4** 5 6 **7** 8 **9** **10**	W WHST . **1** **2** 3 **4** 5 **6** **7** 8 **9** **10**	L LF . 1 2 3 **4** 5 **6**	SL . **1** 2 3 4 5 6
21	RI RH . 1 2 **3** 4 5 6 **7** 8 **9** **10**	W WHST . 1 **2** 3 **4** 5 **6** **7** **8** 9 **10**	L LF . 1 2 3 4 5 6	SL . **1** 2 3 **4** 5 6
22	RI RH . 1 **2** 3 4 **5** 6 **7** **8** **9** **10**	W WHST . 1 **2** 3 **4** 5 6 7 8 9 **10**	L LF . 1 2 3 4 **5** **6**	SL . 1 2 3 4 5 6
23	RI RH . **1** **2** **3** 4 5 6 **7** 8 9 **10**	W WHST . 1 **2** 3 **4** 5 6 7 **8** 9 **10**	L LF . 1 2 3 **4** **5** **6**	SL . 1 2 3 4 5 6
COMPLETE BOOK	RI RH . **1** **2** **3** **4** **5** **6** **7** **8** **9** **10**	W WHST . **1** **2** **3** **4** **5** **6** **7** **8** **9** **10**	L LF . 1 2 3 **4** **5** **6**	SL . **1** **2** 3 **4** **5** **6**

For the complete Common Core standard identifier, combine your grade + "." + letter code above + "." + number code above.

In addition to the correlations indicated here, the activities may be adapted or expanded to align to additional standards and to meet the diverse needs of your unique students!